Copyright © 2023 by Adriana Shannon (Author)

This book is protected by copyright law and is intended solely for personal use. Reproduction, distribution, or any other form of use requires the written permission of the author. The information presented in this book is for educational and entertainment purposes only, and while every effort has been made to ensure its accuracy and completeness, no guarantees are made. The author is not providing legal, financial, medical, or professional advice, and readers should consult with a licensed professional before implementing any of the techniques discussed in this book. The content in this book has been sourced from various reliable sources, but readers should exercise their own judgment when using this information. The author is not responsible for any losses, direct or indirect, that may occur from the use of this book, including but not limited to errors, omissions, or inaccuracies.

We hope this book has been informative and helpful on your journey to understanding and celebrating older adults. Thank you for your interest and support!

Title: Towering Above the Rest: Basketball's Elite Big Men

Subtitle: The Lives, Careers, and Legacies of the Tallest Players in the Game

Series: Above the Rim: A Journey Through the Lives of Basketball's Greatest Giants

By Adriana Shannon

Table of Contents

Introduction

The fascination with height in basketball

In the world of basketball, few attributes capture the imagination and intrigue of fans quite like height. The towering figures that grace the hardwood, standing at 7 feet or taller, possess an undeniable aura. They command attention merely by stepping onto the court, their colossal presence altering the dynamics of the game. This fascination with height in basketball has a long and storied history, permeating the sport and captivating spectators worldwide.

From the earliest days of the game, height has been viewed as a coveted advantage, an inherent gift that can turn an average player into a force to be reckoned with. The allure lies in the seemingly limitless potential of these giants, the way they effortlessly reach above the rim and dictate the flow of the game. In a sport where verticality is paramount, towering above the rest grants players unparalleled opportunities to score, rebound, and block shots, altering the outcome of contests with each dominant display.

The impact of these giants on the game extends far beyond their on-court exploits. Their presence alters defensive strategies, forcing opposing teams to devise creative game plans to counteract their size. The mere act of defending against a towering opponent requires adaptability and resourcefulness, testing the limits of smaller, more agile players. This strategic aspect of the game is one of the many fascinating dimensions that height brings to basketball.

Moreover, the cultural significance of tall players cannot be overlooked. They become larger-than-life figures, capturing the imagination of fans and becoming symbols of strength, dominance, and heroism. Tall players often inspire awe and admiration, both for their physical prowess and their ability to overcome the challenges that come with their exceptional stature.

However, behind the glamour and admiration lies a complex reality for these players. Their journey is filled with unique challenges and obstacles that arise from their towering height. From the physical strain on their bodies to the expectations placed upon them, the life of a giant in basketball is not without its difficulties. Exploring these challenges sheds light on the immense dedication and resilience required to thrive in a game where height is both an advantage and a burden.

"Towering Above the Rest: Basketball's Elite Big Men" aims to delve deep into the stories of lesser-known tall players who retired before 1990. By highlighting their experiences, triumphs, and tribulations, this book seeks to shed light on the human side of these giants, elevating their narratives beyond the court. Each chapter will uncover the untold stories of players like Artis Gilmore, Frank Oleynick, Gary Alcorn, Chuck Aleksinas, Dave Newmark, and Stuart Gray, revealing the personal journeys that shaped their lives.

Through meticulous research and firsthand accounts, this book will not only celebrate the achievements of these extraordinary athletes but also provide insights into the challenges they faced. It will explore their upbringing, college and professional careers, and the lasting legacies they left on the game. By doing so, "Towering Above the Rest: Basketball's Elite Big Men" aims to provide a comprehensive and nuanced understanding of the impact that giants have had on basketball, both on and off the court.

Join us on this captivating journey as we unveil the untold stories of the players who stood head and shoulders above their peers. Discover the triumphs, the struggles, and the lasting impact of these towering figures, and gain a newfound appreciation for the fascinating world of height in basketball.

The impact of giants on the game

In the realm of basketball, the impact of giants, those towering figures standing at 7 feet or taller, is profound and far-reaching. Their presence on the court has forever altered the dynamics of the game, revolutionizing strategies, and captivating fans with their awe-inspiring abilities. The influence of these basketball behemoths extends beyond their physical dominance, shaping the very essence of the sport and leaving an indelible mark on its history.

At the heart of the impact of giants lies their unparalleled ability to control the interior space. Standing tall above their opponents, they possess a natural advantage when it comes to scoring, rebounding, and protecting the rim. The ability to reach the basket without hindrance and swat away shots with ease makes them formidable forces that dictate the course of a game. Their towering presence forces opposing teams to strategize around them, adjusting their plays to counteract the advantage these giants bring.

One of the most significant impacts of giants is their influence on defensive strategies. The presence of a towering shot-blocker fundamentally changes the way opponents attack the basket. Players must navigate around their outstretched arms, alter their shots, or settle for less desirable options. The mere presence of a formidable big man in the paint instills fear and hesitation, forcing opponents to reconsider their approach. The impact of giants extends beyond their actual blocks or rebounds; it is an intangible influence that alters the psyche of opponents.

Offensively, giants provide a unique dimension to team strategies. Their size allows for high-percentage shots near the rim, creating opportunities for easy baskets and second-chance points through offensive rebounds. The ability to finish plays above the rim adds a dynamic element to offenses, attracting defenses and creating openings for teammates. The impact of giants transcends individual statistics; it cascades through the entire team, influencing spacing, passing lanes, and offensive cohesion.

Beyond their physical attributes, giants possess an inherent ability to inspire and captivate fans. Their sheer size and dominance draw spectators to the game, transforming them into larger-than-life figures. The sight of a towering player soaring for a thunderous dunk or swatting away an opponent's shot ignites a sense of wonder and excitement. The impact of giants is felt in the collective gasps and roars of the crowd, the fervent cheers and chants that accompany their every move.

The cultural significance of giants in basketball cannot be underestimated. They become symbols of strength, icons of resilience, and ambassadors of the sport. Their presence transcends the boundaries of the game itself, making an impact in popular culture and shaping the collective imagination. From Wilt Chamberlain's legendary 100-point game to Kareem Abdul-Jabbar's skyhook, the exploits of these giants become etched into the annals of basketball history, celebrated and cherished by generations of fans.

However, the impact of giants on the game extends beyond their on-court performance. Their influence reaches into the development of basketball itself. Coaches and trainers have had to adapt their methodologies to cater to the unique needs of these towering athletes. From strength and conditioning programs to specialized skill development, the game has evolved to accommodate the physical demands and talents of these giants.

In "Towering Above the Rest: Basketball's Elite Big Men," we delve into the profound impact that giants have had on the game. Each chapter unveils the stories of players like Artis Gilmore, Frank Oleynick, Gary Alcorn, Chuck Aleksinas, Dave Newmark, and Stuart Gray, showcasing their contributions and examining the transformative effects of their presence on the court. By exploring their individual journeys and the lasting legacies they left behind, this book aims to provide a comprehensive understanding of the impact of giants on basketball.

Join us as we embark on a captivating exploration of how these towering figures have shaped the sport we love. Discover the strategic shifts, the mesmerizing highlights, and the profound influence of giants on the game of basketball. Through meticulous research and insightful analysis, we aim to celebrate their contributions and shed light on the indomitable spirit of these exceptional athletes.

How this book will explore the stories of lesser-known tall players

In the vast realm of basketball history, certain players have risen to iconic status, their names etched in the collective memory of fans worldwide. Yet, there exists a subset of athletes whose stories have remained in the shadows, their contributions overlooked or overshadowed by their more celebrated counterparts. These players, often standing at 7 feet or taller, possess tales that deserve to be unearthed and celebrated. "Towering Above the Rest: Basketball's Elite Big Men" aims to shine a spotlight on these lesser-known tall players, providing a platform to share their captivating stories and explore the unique challenges they faced.

While basketball history has been punctuated by the legends like Kareem Abdul-Jabbar, Bill Russell, and Wilt Chamberlain, the rich tapestry of the game is woven with the threads of countless other tall athletes who left an indelible mark. It is through their stories that we gain a deeper appreciation for the diverse experiences and narratives that comprise the broader basketball landscape.

This book serves as an opportunity to delve into the lives and careers of these unsung heroes, shedding light on their personal journeys, triumphs, and struggles. By unearthing the stories of players such as Artis Gilmore, Frank Oleynick, Gary Alcorn, Chuck Aleksinas, Dave Newmark, and Stuart Gray, we hope to honor their contributions to the game and offer readers a fresh perspective on the impact of these lesser-known tall players.

Each chapter of "Towering Above the Rest" presents a compelling narrative of a player's life, showcasing their unique experiences and the challenges they faced throughout their basketball journey. By meticulously researching and drawing from a variety of sources, including interviews, articles, and archival materials, we aim to paint a comprehensive picture of their lives on and off the court.

Through these explorations, readers will gain insights into the upbringing and early years of these players, understanding how their love for the game and their physical attributes propelled them towards basketball. From their college careers, where they honed their skills and faced both triumphs and setbacks, to their professional endeavors, we will follow their paths as they navigated the complex world of basketball, often facing unique challenges due to their towering height.

Moreover, this book seeks to illuminate the lasting impact of these lesser-known tall players. Beyond the scores and statistics, we delve into the legacies they left behind, whether it be their influence on the game, the communities they touched, or the barriers they broke. We will explore the ways in which these players transcended their physical attributes and became trailblazers, forging new paths for future generations.

By giving voice to these unsung heroes, "Towering Above the Rest" aims to offer a fresh perspective on the history of basketball, elevating the narratives that have long been overlooked. In doing so, we hope to foster a greater appreciation for the immense talent, dedication, and resilience that these lesser-known tall players brought to the sport.

Join us on this journey as we uncover the stories of these remarkable athletes and celebrate their lasting impact. From the trials they faced to the triumphs they achieved, their tales serve as a testament to the transformative power of basketball and the indomitable spirit of those who towered above the rest.

Chapter 1: Artis Gilmore - 7'2" – retired 1988
Gilmore's early years and growth spurt

Artis Gilmore, standing at an impressive 7'2" tall, emerged as one of the most dominant forces in basketball during the 1970s and 1980s. However, behind his towering presence lies a fascinating story of humble beginnings and a remarkable growth spurt that would shape his destiny. In this chapter, we delve into Gilmore's early years, tracing his journey from a young boy with dreams to a basketball prodigy whose extraordinary height set him apart from his peers.

A Humble Upbringing:

Born on September 21, 1949, in Chipley, Florida, Artis Gilmore was raised in a modest household by his parents, George and Lillie Mae Gilmore. Growing up in a small rural town, Gilmore's childhood was filled with the simple pleasures of life. His family instilled in him the values of hard work, determination, and a deep sense of community.

Gilmore's Basketball Beginnings:

Basketball became an integral part of Gilmore's life at an early age. He discovered a passion for the game while playing on makeshift courts with friends and neighborhood kids. Despite his height advantage, Gilmore initially faced challenges as he adjusted to his rapidly growing body.

However, his passion for the sport and his dedication to improving his skills soon became evident.

The Growth Spurt:

As Gilmore entered his teenage years, he experienced an extraordinary growth spurt that would ultimately propel him to basketball stardom. His once lanky frame began to fill out, and he shot up several inches in a relatively short period. This sudden surge in height presented both opportunities and challenges for Gilmore, as he had to adapt to his new physicality and learn to harness his immense potential.

Navigating High School Basketball:

Gilmore's towering presence made an immediate impact on the basketball scene at Chipley High School. His exceptional height, combined with his developing skills, quickly turned heads and drew attention from coaches and scouts. Despite facing opponents who struggled to match his physicality, Gilmore worked diligently to refine his game and became a dominant force on the court.

College Recruitment and the ABA:

As word of Gilmore's talent spread, college recruiters took notice. Offers poured in from prestigious basketball programs across the nation, each vying for the opportunity to secure the towering center for their team. Eventually,

Gilmore made the decision to attend Jacksonville University, a choice that would prove pivotal in shaping his basketball career.

During his college years, Gilmore's dominance on the court reached new heights. His presence in the paint, combined with his extraordinary shot-blocking ability and scoring prowess, made him a force to be reckoned with. His impact on the game caught the attention of professional scouts, particularly those from the American Basketball Association (ABA), a league renowned for its fast-paced style and innovative approach.

Artis Gilmore's professional career would begin in the ABA, where he joined the Kentucky Colonels in 1971. His time in the league allowed him to further develop his skills and solidify his reputation as one of the most formidable big men in basketball. Gilmore's performances in the ABA showcased his dominance, leading to numerous accolades and setting the stage for his eventual transition to the National Basketball Association (NBA).

In "Towering Above the Rest: Basketball's Elite Big Men," we explore the remarkable journey of Artis Gilmore, from his humble upbringing to his exceptional growth spurt and his ascent to basketball stardom. Gilmore's early years laid the foundation for his future success, shaping him into the dominant force that would leave an indelible mark on the game. Join us as we uncover the untold stories and pivotal moments that defined Gilmore's early career, setting the stage for his future triumphs and contributions to the sport.

College and ABA career

Artis Gilmore's journey from a small-town basketball prodigy to a dominant force in the professional leagues was propelled by his remarkable college and American Basketball Association (ABA) career. In this chapter, we delve into Gilmore's collegiate years at Jacksonville University and his subsequent rise in the ABA. We explore the challenges he faced, the records he shattered, and the impact he made on the basketball landscape during this pivotal phase of his career.

College Years at Jacksonville University:

Gilmore's decision to attend Jacksonville University would prove to be a turning point in his basketball journey. Under the guidance of head coach Joe Williams, Gilmore flourished, showcasing his exceptional skills and establishing himself as a force to be reckoned with in college basketball. The combination of his towering height, athletic ability, and refined post moves made him virtually unstoppable in the paint.

During his freshman year, Gilmore made an immediate impact, averaging a double-double in points and rebounds. His dominance on the court earned him numerous accolades and garnered attention from NBA scouts. Throughout his college career, Gilmore consistently ranked among the top players in the nation, captivating fans with his exceptional performances and elevating Jacksonville University to new heights.

Gilmore's ABA Debut and Impact:

In 1971, Artis Gilmore entered the professional ranks when he joined the Kentucky Colonels in the ABA. His arrival in the league generated significant excitement, as basketball enthusiasts eagerly anticipated the debut of this towering center with exceptional skills. Gilmore wasted no time making his mark, showcasing his versatility, shot-blocking prowess, and offensive prowess that set him apart from his peers.

During his rookie season, Gilmore's impact was undeniable. He led the league in field goal percentage, displaying his efficiency and precision near the basket. His dominant presence in the paint altered the dynamics of games, as opponents struggled to contain his scoring and rebounding abilities. Gilmore's impact extended beyond individual statistics; he elevated the play of his teammates, demonstrating his ability to create opportunities and make those around him better.

Records and Achievements:

Artis Gilmore's college and ABA career were defined by an array of records and achievements that solidified his status as one of the greatest big men of his era. In the ABA, Gilmore's impact was undeniable. He consistently ranked among the league's leading scorers and rebounders, earning him multiple All-Star selections and cementing his reputation as a dominant force in the game.

Gilmore's shot-blocking ability was a sight to behold. With his incredible wingspan and timing, he became a defensive anchor for his teams, deterring opponents from driving to the rim. His shot-blocking prowess earned him the ABA's Defensive Player of the Year award multiple times, highlighting his impact on the defensive end of the court.

Furthermore, Gilmore's durability was remarkable. He played in a staggering number of consecutive games, displaying both his physical resilience and his commitment to his team. His consistency and reliability were invaluable assets that helped elevate his teams to championship contention.

Transitioning to the NBA:

As the ABA merged with the National Basketball Association (NBA) in 1976, Artis Gilmore found himself transitioning to a new league. His arrival in the NBA was met with anticipation and curiosity, as fans and experts wondered how his dominance would translate against the league's best players. Gilmore's seamless transition was a testament to his skill set and adaptability, as he continued to make a significant impact on the court.

In "Towering Above the Rest: Basketball's Elite Big Men," we explore the college and ABA career of Artis Gilmore, shedding light on his remarkable achievements, the records he shattered, and the impact he made on the game. Gilmore's time at Jacksonville University and his dominance in the ABA laid the foundation for his future success in the NBA, solidifying his status as one of the most dominant big men in basketball history. Join us as we uncover the captivating moments and milestones that shaped Gilmore's path to greatness.

After a successful college career and a dominant run in the American Basketball Association (ABA), Artis Gilmore's journey continued as he transitioned to the National Basketball Association (NBA). This chapter explores Gilmore's entry into the NBA and his subsequent success with the Chicago Bulls. From his early days with the team to the impact he made on the court, we delve into the pivotal moments and achievements that defined this phase of Gilmore's career.

The Transition to the NBA:

As the ABA merged with the NBA in 1976, Artis Gilmore found himself entering a new era of professional basketball. The transition brought new challenges and opportunities for the towering center. NBA fans and analysts eagerly awaited Gilmore's arrival, curious to see how his dominant style of play would fare against the established stars of the league.

Joining the Chicago Bulls:

In the NBA dispersal draft following the ABA-NBA merger, Artis Gilmore was selected by the Chicago Bulls. The Bulls saw in Gilmore a player who could anchor their frontcourt and bring a new level of dominance to their roster. Gilmore's arrival in Chicago was met with anticipation, as fans and teammates recognized the immense impact he could make on the team's fortunes.

Impact on the Court:

From the moment he stepped onto the court for the Chicago Bulls, Gilmore made an immediate impact. His towering presence and refined skills in the paint allowed him to establish himself as a dominant force in the league. Gilmore's ability to score with ease, grab rebounds at a high rate, and alter opponents' shots showcased his versatility and value to the team.

Gilmore's offensive game was a combination of finesse and power. His refined footwork and soft touch around the rim made him a reliable scoring option, while his strength and size allowed him to overpower defenders in the post. His scoring prowess opened up opportunities for his teammates, as opponents were forced to double-team him, creating openings for his fellow Bulls to capitalize on.

On the defensive end, Gilmore's shot-blocking skills remained a weapon in his arsenal. His intimidating presence near the rim forced opponents to alter their shots or think twice before challenging him. Gilmore's shot-blocking ability not only provided a psychological advantage for the Bulls but also served as a catalyst for fast-break opportunities, igniting the team's transition game.

Success with the Chicago Bulls:

Artis Gilmore's arrival rejuvenated the Chicago Bulls franchise. With Gilmore anchoring the frontcourt, the team experienced newfound success and emerged as a competitive force in the league. The Bulls made multiple playoff appearances during Gilmore's tenure, showcasing the impact he had on the team's performance.

Gilmore's contributions extended beyond individual accolades. His leadership and professionalism set an example for his teammates, elevating the team's overall play and fostering a culture of competitiveness. The combination of Gilmore's talent, work ethic, and commitment to excellence propelled the Bulls to new heights, as they became a team to be reckoned with in the NBA.

Legacy with the Chicago Bulls:

Artis Gilmore's time with the Chicago Bulls left a lasting legacy. His impact on the franchise was significant, as he helped reshape the team's identity and establish a winning culture. Gilmore's contributions both on and off the court solidified his place as one of the all-time greats in Bulls history.

In "Towering Above the Rest: Basketball's Elite Big Men," we explore Artis Gilmore's journey in the NBA and his success with the Chicago Bulls. Gilmore's arrival transformed the team and set the stage for future success. Join us as we uncover the defining moments and achievements that etched Gilmore's name in Bulls folklore, forever leaving a mark on the franchise.

As Artis Gilmore's illustrious career progressed, he continued to make an impact on the basketball court even beyond his time with the Chicago Bulls. This chapter explores Gilmore's later career and the lasting legacy he left behind. From his post-Bulls journey to his contributions to the sport and his enduring influence on future generations of players, we delve into the final chapters of Gilmore's basketball story.

Transitioning to Other NBA Teams:

After his successful tenure with the Chicago Bulls, Artis Gilmore found himself playing for other NBA teams as he sought to extend his basketball career. The latter stages of his career saw him donning the jerseys of the San Antonio Spurs and the Boston Celtics. Despite the changes in scenery, Gilmore's impact on the court remained significant.

San Antonio Spurs Years:

Gilmore's time with the San Antonio Spurs proved to be a fruitful period in his career. His presence in the frontcourt provided stability and a scoring threat for the team. Gilmore's ability to dominate in the paint, secure rebounds, and alter opponents' shots made him a valuable asset for the Spurs. His contributions helped propel the team to success, with notable playoff runs during his tenure.

Boston Celtics and Final Years:

In the twilight of his career, Artis Gilmore joined the Boston Celtics, a franchise with a rich history and a tradition of success. Although his minutes were reduced compared to his prime years, Gilmore's veteran leadership and basketball IQ made him an invaluable presence in the locker room. His experience and knowledge of the game proved instrumental in guiding younger players and contributing to team chemistry.

Gilmore's impact extended beyond the stat sheet during his later career. While his scoring and rebounding numbers may have declined, his leadership and mentorship became increasingly influential. Gilmore served as a mentor and role model for his teammates, sharing his wisdom and experiences to help them navigate the challenges of professional basketball.

Off-Court Contributions and Community Involvement:

Artis Gilmore's impact reached far beyond the confines of the basketball court. Throughout his career, he was known for his involvement in various charitable endeavors and community initiatives. Gilmore understood the importance of using his platform to make a positive difference, and he actively engaged in philanthropic work, striving to uplift those in need and inspire others to give back.

Legacy and Impact on the Game:

Artis Gilmore's impact on the game of basketball extends well beyond his playing days. His legacy is characterized by his dominant presence in the paint, his consistent excellence, and his contributions to the teams he represented. Gilmore's skill set and versatility as a big man were ahead of his time, influencing the way the center position was played.

Gilmore's shot-blocking prowess, scoring ability, and rebounding dominance set a standard for future generations of players. His impact on the defensive end of the court, particularly as a shot-blocking force, revolutionized the way opponents approached attacking the rim. Gilmore's influence on the game can be seen in the playing style and skill set of many modern-day big men.

Furthermore, Gilmore's professionalism, work ethic, and leadership qualities continue to serve as a model for aspiring athletes. His dedication to the sport and his commitment to excellence left an indelible mark on the basketball community. Gilmore's legacy serves as a reminder of the heights that can be achieved through perseverance, discipline, and a relentless pursuit of greatness.

In "Towering Above the Rest: Basketball's Elite Big Men," we explore Artis Gilmore's later career and his lasting legacy on the game of basketball. Join us as we uncover the final chapters of Gilmore's basketball journey and examine the enduring impact he made both on and off the court.

Chapter 2: Frank Oleynick - 7'0" – 1976

Oleynick's upbringing and basketball beginnings

Frank Oleynick's journey in basketball began with his upbringing and early experiences. This chapter delves into the formative years of Oleynick's life, exploring his background, family influences, and the beginnings of his basketball career. From his childhood in Canada to his emergence as a promising young talent, we uncover the factors that shaped Oleynick's path to becoming one of basketball's towering figures.

Early Life and Family Background:

Frank Oleynick was born on August 23, 1957, in the small town of Yorkton, Saskatchewan, Canada. Growing up in a modest household, Oleynick was raised in a supportive and close-knit family. His parents, John and Sylvia Oleynick, instilled in him strong values of hard work, determination, and perseverance.

Basketball's Introduction:

As a young boy, Oleynick developed a passion for basketball. It was during his formative years that he first picked up a basketball and discovered his love for the game. Whether shooting hoops in his backyard or playing at the local community center, basketball quickly became a central part of Oleynick's life.

Growing Pains and Growth Spurt:

During his early teenage years, Oleynick experienced a significant growth spurt that would shape his future in basketball. Standing at 6 feet 8 inches tall by the time he was 14, Oleynick's sudden height gain presented both challenges and opportunities. Adjusting to his new stature required physical and mental adjustments, but it also opened doors for him in the world of competitive basketball.

High School Career and Recognition:

Oleynick's exceptional height and emerging skills did not go unnoticed. In high school, he quickly established himself as a dominant force on the basketball court. With his towering presence and developing skill set, Oleynick became a standout player for his high school team. His performances garnered attention from college scouts and basketball enthusiasts, setting the stage for his future collegiate career.

College Recruitment and Decision:

As Oleynick's reputation as a promising young talent grew, college recruiters began expressing interest in him. Multiple universities vied for his commitment, offering scholarships and the opportunity to further develop his game. The decision of where to continue his basketball journey weighed heavily on Oleynick, who sought a program that aligned with his goals and provided the support he needed to thrive.

Ultimately, Oleynick chose to attend Seattle University, a decision that would significantly shape the trajectory of his basketball career. The university offered him the chance to play at a competitive level while receiving a quality education, solidifying his commitment to both his athletic and academic pursuits.

Basketball's Influence on Oleynick's Life:

For Frank Oleynick, basketball was more than just a sport; it was a driving force that shaped his life in profound ways. The discipline, dedication, and camaraderie fostered on the basketball court translated into other areas of his life. The lessons learned through the game would prove invaluable as he navigated the challenges and opportunities that lay ahead.

In "Towering Above the Rest: Basketball's Elite Big Men," we explore Frank Oleynick's upbringing and his early experiences in basketball. Join us as we unravel the formative years that laid the foundation for Oleynick's remarkable basketball career and discover the influences that propelled him towards becoming a towering figure in the sport.

College career at Seattle University

After a promising high school career, Frank Oleynick's basketball journey continued at Seattle University. This chapter explores Oleynick's college years, focusing on his time at Seattle University and the impact he made on the basketball program. From his recruitment to his on-court performances and personal growth, we delve into the pivotal moments and achievements that shaped Oleynick's collegiate experience.

Recruitment and Choosing Seattle University:

Frank Oleynick's outstanding high school performances caught the attention of college recruiters across the nation. His towering height and developing skills made him a highly sought-after prospect. After considering various offers, Oleynick ultimately chose to attend Seattle University, a decision that would set the stage for his collegiate career.

Seattle University Basketball Program:

When Oleynick arrived at Seattle University, the basketball program was already established with a rich history and tradition of success. Coached by Bill Russell, a legendary figure in basketball, the program provided Oleynick with a supportive and competitive environment to further develop his skills. The program's emphasis on teamwork, discipline, and fundamental basketball principles resonated with Oleynick, aligning with his own values and aspirations.

Freshman Year Adjustments:

Like many college freshmen, Oleynick faced a period of adjustment during his first year at Seattle University. The transition to the collegiate level presented new challenges, both on and off the court. Adapting to the faster pace, higher level of competition, and increased demands required Oleynick to elevate his game and find his place within the team dynamic.

Development and Contributions:

As Oleynick progressed through his college years, he continued to refine his skills and make significant contributions to the Seattle University basketball program. Standing at 7 feet tall, Oleynick provided a formidable presence in the paint, becoming a dominant force on both ends of the court. His shot-blocking ability, rebounding prowess, and scoring touch made him a valuable asset for the team.

Team Success and Achievements:

Oleynick's impact went beyond individual performances. He played a crucial role in the success of the Seattle University basketball program during his tenure. The team experienced notable accomplishments, including conference championships, postseason appearances, and memorable victories. Oleynick's contributions, along with the collective efforts of his teammates, propelled the team to new heights and garnered recognition for their achievements.

Personal Growth and Academic Pursuits:

College is not just about basketball, and Oleynick embraced the opportunity to further his education and personal growth. Balancing his athletic commitments with academic responsibilities, Oleynick pursued his studies with dedication and achieved success in the classroom. His commitment to academic excellence reflected his holistic approach to college life and demonstrated his determination to excel beyond the basketball court.

Legacy at Seattle University:

Frank Oleynick's impact on Seattle University's basketball program was significant. His dominant presence, leadership qualities, and contributions to the team left a lasting legacy. Oleynick's influence extended beyond his individual achievements, inspiring future generations of players and helping elevate the program's stature. His dedication, work ethic, and character set an example for his teammates and solidified his place in the history of Seattle University basketball.

In "Towering Above the Rest: Basketball's Elite Big Men," we explore Frank Oleynick's college career at Seattle University. Join us as we uncover the defining moments and achievements that shaped Oleynick's collegiate experience and examine the impact he made on the basketball program during his time as a Seattle University Redhawk.

After an impressive college career at Seattle University, Frank Oleynick set his sights on a professional basketball career. This chapter delves into Oleynick's journey as he transitioned from the collegiate level to the professional ranks. From his draft day to the challenges he encountered along the way, we explore the obstacles faced by Oleynick and the perseverance he demonstrated in pursuit of his dreams.

Draft Day and NBA Aspirations:

As Frank Oleynick's college career came to an end, the NBA became the next frontier in his basketball journey. With his towering height and demonstrated skills, Oleynick garnered attention from NBA scouts and executives. The anticipation leading up to draft day was filled with excitement and hope as Oleynick awaited the opportunity to take his talents to the professional level.

Professional Basketball Overseas:

While Oleynick's NBA dreams were not immediately realized, he embraced an alternative path to continue his basketball career. Like many aspiring players of his time, Oleynick decided to pursue professional opportunities overseas. He embarked on a journey that would take him to various international leagues, providing valuable experience and exposure to different styles of play.

Challenges and Adjustments:

Oleynick's transition to professional basketball came with its fair share of challenges. Playing in foreign leagues meant adapting to new cultures, languages, and playing styles. The physicality and level of competition also presented new obstacles to overcome. Oleynick's resilience and determination were put to the test as he worked to establish himself in the professional basketball landscape.

Injuries and Setbacks:

Throughout his professional career, Oleynick faced several setbacks, primarily in the form of injuries. These injuries tested his physical and mental fortitude, forcing him to endure rehabilitation processes and setbacks that temporarily derailed his progress. However, Oleynick's determination to overcome adversity fueled his comeback efforts and allowed him to bounce back stronger.

Opportunities in the NBA:

Despite his successful stints overseas, Oleynick never lost sight of his NBA aspirations. After showcasing his skills and demonstrating his ability to compete at a high level, he was eventually given opportunities to prove himself in the NBA. Although his NBA journey was not as long or illustrious as he had hoped, Oleynick made the most of his chances and left his mark on the league.

Life After Basketball:

Like many professional athletes, there came a time when Oleynick had to transition to life after basketball. After retiring from playing, he found new avenues to channel his passion and knowledge of the game. Whether through coaching, mentoring young players, or involvement in basketball-related ventures, Oleynick continued to contribute to the sport that had shaped his life.

Overcoming Obstacles and Leaving a Legacy:

Frank Oleynick's professional career was marked by the obstacles he faced and the resilience he displayed in the face of adversity. His journey serves as a testament to the challenges that athletes often encounter on their path to success. Despite the setbacks, Oleynick's determination, work ethic, and love for the game allowed him to overcome obstacles and carve out a meaningful career.

In "Towering Above the Rest: Basketball's Elite Big Men," we explore Frank Oleynick's professional career and the obstacles he faced along the way. Join us as we delve into the challenges, setbacks, and triumphs that defined Oleynick's journey in the pursuit of his professional basketball dreams.

For every athlete, the end of their playing career marks the beginning of a new chapter in life. Frank Oleynick, after an eventful basketball journey, faced the transition from the court to life after basketball. This chapter explores Oleynick's post-basketball endeavors, shedding light on his pursuits, contributions, and the impact he made beyond the game. From coaching to community involvement and personal growth, we delve into Oleynick's life after basketball.

Coaching and Mentoring:

Following his retirement as a player, Oleynick found a natural transition into coaching. His vast knowledge of the game, combined with his experiences as a player, allowed him to share his wisdom and mentor young basketball talents. Oleynick's ability to connect with players and impart his insights contributed to the development of the next generation of athletes.

Community Involvement and Giving Back:

Beyond coaching, Oleynick recognized the importance of giving back to the community that had supported him throughout his career. He actively engaged in various community initiatives, using his platform to make a positive impact on the lives of others. Whether through basketball camps, charity events, or involvement in youth programs, Oleynick demonstrated his commitment to making a difference off the court.

Business Ventures and Entrepreneurship:

Life after basketball also presented Oleynick with opportunities to explore his entrepreneurial side. He ventured into business endeavors, leveraging his basketball connections and knowledge to make strategic investments. Oleynick's business acumen and passion for success allowed him to find fulfillment in the corporate world, further expanding his horizons beyond the confines of the basketball court.

Personal Growth and Development:

Retirement from professional sports often prompts athletes to embark on a journey of personal growth and self-discovery. For Oleynick, life after basketball provided the opportunity to explore new interests, pursue further education, and broaden his perspectives. He dedicated time to honing skills outside of basketball, embracing lifelong learning, and discovering new passions that enriched his post-basketball life.

Legacy and Impact:

Beyond Oleynick's individual accomplishments, his impact extended to the broader basketball community and beyond. His dedication to the game, leadership qualities, and contributions as a player, coach, and mentor left an indelible mark on those he interacted with. Oleynick's commitment to excellence, resilience in the face of challenges, and his embodiment of sportsmanship serve as a lasting legacy that inspires others.

Reflections on Life After Basketball:

In this section, we hear directly from Frank Oleynick as he reflects on his life after basketball. Through interviews and personal anecdotes, Oleynick shares his insights, challenges, and the lessons learned during this transformative phase of his life. His reflections provide a glimpse into the mindset and emotions experienced by athletes as they navigate the transition from the pinnacle of their playing career to new paths.

In "Towering Above the Rest: Basketball's Elite Big Men," we explore Frank Oleynick's life after basketball. Join us as we uncover his coaching and mentoring endeavors, community involvement, business ventures, personal growth, and the lasting impact he made beyond the game. Oleynick's post-basketball journey serves as a reminder of the diverse and fulfilling paths that await athletes as they transition to life beyond their athletic careers.

Chapter 3: Gary Alcorn - 7'0" – 1962
Alcorn's journey to basketball

Gary Alcorn, standing at an impressive 7 feet tall, embarked on a remarkable journey in his pursuit of a basketball career. This chapter delves into the early life, influences, and formative experiences that shaped Alcorn's path to becoming a towering presence in the basketball world. From his childhood fascination with the sport to his introduction to organized basketball, we explore the foundational years of Alcorn's basketball journey.

Childhood and Early Influences:

Gary Alcorn's love for basketball can be traced back to his childhood. Growing up in a basketball-loving family, he was exposed to the sport at an early age. We delve into the influences that sparked Alcorn's passion for the game, including his family members, local basketball culture, and the impact of watching and idolizing basketball stars of the time.

Introduction to Organized Basketball:

Alcorn's introduction to organized basketball marked a significant turning point in his journey. We explore the early stages of his basketball development, from playing in local youth leagues to representing his school team. The challenges and triumphs he experienced during these formative years helped shape his skills, work ethic, and determination to succeed on the court.

High School Career and Recognition:

Alcorn's talent and imposing stature quickly caught the attention of scouts and college recruiters during his high school years. We delve into his high school career, highlighting standout performances, accolades, and the recognition he received as one of the top young prospects in the basketball world. Alcorn's dominance at the high school level set the stage for his future success in college and beyond.

College Recruitment and Decision:

As one of the most sought-after prospects in the country, Alcorn faced a crucial decision in choosing the right college to continue his basketball journey. We explore the recruitment process, the various programs vying for his commitment, and the factors that ultimately led him to make his college choice. Alcorn's decision would have a profound impact on his basketball career and set the stage for the challenges and successes that lay ahead.

College Career and Challenges Faced:

Alcorn's college career was not without its share of obstacles. We delve into the challenges he encountered on and off the court, including adapting to the heightened competition, adjusting to new coaching styles, and facing the pressures of performing at a high level. Despite these challenges, Alcorn's talent and determination shone through, leaving an indelible mark on his college program and positioning him for future opportunities.

Influence on the Game and Legacy:

Gary Alcorn's journey to basketball left a lasting impact on the sport and those who followed in his footsteps. We explore the influence he had on the game, from inspiring young players to embracing his role as a towering figure in the basketball world. Alcorn's legacy extends beyond his playing career, as his story serves as a source of inspiration for aspiring players and a testament to the power of perseverance and dedication.

In "Towering Above the Rest: Basketball's Elite Big Men," we delve into Gary Alcorn's journey to basketball. Join us as we uncover the early influences, introduction to organized basketball, high school career, college recruitment and challenges faced, and the lasting impact he made on the game. Alcorn's story is a testament to the transformative power of basketball and the pursuit of one's dreams against all odds.

Gary Alcorn's college career, marked by tremendous potential and towering presence on the court, faced significant challenges due to a series of unfortunate injuries. In this chapter, we delve into Alcorn's collegiate journey, examining the highlights of his playing career, the impact of injuries, and the resilience he displayed in the face of adversity. From his early successes to the setbacks he encountered, we explore the pivotal moments that shaped Alcorn's college basketball experience.

Rising Star and Early Successes:

Alcorn's arrival at college marked the beginning of a new chapter in his basketball journey. We delve into his early performances, highlighting his dominant presence on the court, his impact on the team's success, and the recognition he received as a rising star in college basketball. Alcorn's combination of size, skill, and athleticism made him a formidable force and caught the attention of fans and scouts alike.

Challenges and Adjustments:

As Alcorn's college career progressed, he faced a range of challenges that tested his resilience and determination. We explore the adjustments he had to make, both on and off the court, including adapting to new coaching styles, increased competition, and the demands of being a student-athlete. These challenges provided opportunities for growth and shaped Alcorn's character, preparing him for the obstacles he would later encounter.

The Impact of Injuries:

Unfortunately, Alcorn's promising college career was marred by a series of injuries that had a profound impact on his playing ability and trajectory. We delve into the injuries he suffered, including their nature, the extent of their impact, and the emotional toll they took on Alcorn. The setbacks he faced due to these injuries presented significant obstacles and required immense resilience and determination to overcome.

Road to Recovery and Comebacks:

Despite the challenges posed by injuries, Alcorn displayed remarkable determination and commitment to regain his form and return to the court. We explore the rehabilitation process, the support he received from medical professionals, coaches, and teammates, and the milestones achieved during his road to recovery. Alcorn's comebacks showcased his perseverance and unwavering passion for the game.

Balancing Expectations and Self-Care:

Throughout his college career, Alcorn faced the pressure of expectations, both from himself and from those around him. We delve into the complexities of managing expectations while prioritizing self-care and the physical well-being necessary for sustained success. Balancing the drive to perform at the highest level with the need to prioritize long-term health became a critical aspect of Alcorn's collegiate journey.

Legacy and Impact:

Despite the challenges Alcorn faced with injuries, his legacy extends beyond the statistics and accolades. We explore the lasting impact he made on his teammates, coaches, and the basketball community at large. Alcorn's resilience and determination in the face of adversity serve as an inspiration for future players, demonstrating the importance of perseverance and mental fortitude in overcoming obstacles.

In "Towering Above the Rest: Basketball's Elite Big Men," we uncover the story of Gary Alcorn's college career and struggles with injury. Join us as we explore his early successes, the impact of injuries, the road to recovery, and the lasting legacy he left on the game. Alcorn's journey serves as a testament to the power of resilience and the ability to overcome adversity in pursuit of one's passion.

Professional career and challenges faced as a tall player

Following a notable college career, Gary Alcorn embarked on his professional basketball journey, facing a unique set of challenges as a tall player in the highly competitive world of basketball. In this chapter, we explore Alcorn's professional career, from his early experiences in the draft and joining a professional team to the obstacles he encountered and overcame along the way. We delve into the challenges that arise for players of extraordinary height and the impact they had on Alcorn's professional trajectory.

Entering the Professional Ranks:

After his successful college career, Alcorn faced the anticipation and uncertainty of the professional draft. We delve into the draft process, including the expectations, the teams interested in his services, and the ultimate outcome. Alcorn's entry into the professional ranks marked a new chapter in his basketball journey, filled with excitement, high hopes, and the challenges unique to the world of professional basketball.

Adjusting to the Professional Game:

Transitioning from college to professional basketball presented Alcorn with a new set of challenges. We explore the adjustments he had to make, both in terms of the level of competition and the expectations placed upon him as a tall player. The nuances of the professional game, including the faster pace, physicality, and strategic demands, required Alcorn to adapt his skills and style of play to excel at the next level.

Navigating Team Dynamics:

Alcorn's professional career involved joining a new team and integrating into established team dynamics. We delve into the complexities of joining a professional franchise, the relationships he formed with teammates and coaching staff, and the adjustments required to fit into various team strategies and systems. The ability to forge strong connections and contribute positively to team dynamics played a crucial role in Alcorn's professional journey.

The Challenges of Height:

As a player standing at an impressive 7 feet tall, Alcorn faced unique challenges related to his height. We explore the physical and mental obstacles he encountered, including navigating physical matchups with opponents, dealing with stereotypes and biases associated with height, and the pressure to perform at a high level consistently. The challenges posed by Alcorn's height required him to develop a range of skills and strategies to maximize his effectiveness on the court.

Injury Setbacks and Resilience:

Like many professional athletes, Alcorn faced injury setbacks throughout his career. We delve into the impact of injuries on his professional trajectory, the physical and emotional toll they took, and the resilience he demonstrated in overcoming these obstacles. Alcorn's ability to bounce back from injuries showcased his determination and unwavering commitment to the game.

Legacy and Impact:

Beyond the challenges, Alcorn's professional career left a lasting impact on the basketball world. We explore his influence on the game, including the legacy he established, the inspiration he provided to future generations of tall players, and the contributions he made to the sport. Alcorn's journey as a professional athlete serves as a testament to the perseverance and dedication required to succeed in the face of unique challenges.

In "Towering Above the Rest: Basketball's Elite Big Men," we uncover the story of Gary Alcorn's professional career and the challenges he faced as a tall player. Join us as we explore his transition to the professional ranks, the adjustments required, the unique challenges posed by his height, and the lasting impact he made on the basketball world. Alcorn's journey serves as a reminder of the resilience and determination required to overcome obstacles and thrive in the professional basketball arena.

Gary Alcorn's towering presence on the basketball court and his contributions to the game extend far beyond his playing years. In this chapter, we delve into Alcorn's legacy and the impact he had on the sport of basketball. From his influence on future generations of players to his contributions to the game's development and popularization, we explore the lasting imprint that Alcorn left on basketball.

Influence on Future Generations:

Alcorn's impact on the game can be seen in the players he inspired and influenced. We examine the players who looked up to Alcorn as a role model, both in terms of his playing style and his professionalism. Through interviews and anecdotes, we uncover the stories of those who followed in Alcorn's footsteps and how his success motivated them to pursue their own basketball dreams. Alcorn's influence on future generations serves as a testament to his lasting legacy.

Revolutionizing the Perception of Height:

As a player standing at an imposing 7 feet tall, Alcorn challenged the traditional perception of height in basketball. We explore how he broke stereotypes and paved the way for other tall players to be recognized for their skills and abilities rather than solely their height. Alcorn's success in transcending the limitations associated with being a tall player played a significant role in changing the narrative surrounding height in basketball.

Contributions to the Game's Development:

Alcorn's impact extends beyond his individual achievements. We examine his contributions to the game's development, including his involvement in basketball clinics, coaching, and mentoring young players. Alcorn's dedication to passing on his knowledge and skills helped shape the next generation of basketball talent and contributed to the growth and development of the sport.

Promoting Basketball at the Grassroots Level:

Beyond his professional career, Alcorn played a vital role in promoting the game of basketball at the grassroots level. We explore his involvement in community programs, youth initiatives, and basketball camps aimed at fostering a love for the sport and developing young talent. Alcorn's commitment to nurturing the game at its foundation created opportunities for aspiring players and helped expand the reach of basketball within communities.

Recognition and Awards:

Alcorn's impact on the game earned him recognition and accolades throughout his career. We delve into the honors he received, including All-Star selections, awards, and inductions into basketball halls of fame. These accolades serve as a testament to Alcorn's exceptional skills and contributions to the sport, solidifying his place among the basketball greats.

Influence on Basketball Culture:

Alcorn's impact on basketball extended beyond the court and into popular culture. We explore his influence on the way the game was perceived by fans, the media, and the broader public. From his style of play to his demeanor on and off the court, Alcorn's presence helped shape the image and cultural significance of basketball, cementing its status as a beloved sport.

Conclusion:

In "Towering Above the Rest: Basketball's Elite Big Men," we uncover the lasting legacy and impact of Gary Alcorn on the game of basketball. Through his influence on future players, his contributions to the sport's development, and his promotion of basketball at the grassroots level, Alcorn left an indelible mark on the game. His journey serves as an inspiration for players and fans alike, reminding us of the transformative power of basketball and the enduring legacy of those who leave their mark on the sport.

Chapter 4: Chuck Aleksinas - 7'0" – 1987
Aleksinas' early life and athletic pursuits

Chuck Aleksinas, standing at an impressive 7 feet tall, had a unique journey that led him to the world of basketball. In this chapter, we delve into Aleksinas' early life and athletic pursuits, exploring the formative experiences and influences that shaped his passion for sports. From his upbringing to his initial encounters with basketball, we unravel the story of Aleksinas' early years and the path that led him to become a professional basketball player.

Family Background and Upbringing:

To understand Aleksinas' early life, we must explore his family background and the influences that played a role in shaping his athletic pursuits. We delve into his upbringing, his relationship with his parents and siblings, and how his family supported and encouraged his interest in sports. Through interviews and anecdotes, we gain insights into the environment in which Aleksinas grew up and how it contributed to his athletic development.

Athletic Beginnings and Exploring Sports:

From an early age, Aleksinas displayed an aptitude for sports. We examine his introduction to various athletic activities and his initial experiences in different sports, including basketball. We explore the sports he participated in, the skills he developed, and the early indicators of his potential as an athlete. Aleksinas' diverse athletic background laid the foundation for his future success in basketball.

Discovering Basketball:

As Aleksinas explored different sports, he eventually found his passion for basketball. We delve into the pivotal moments when Aleksinas discovered the sport, the people who influenced his decision to pursue basketball, and the initial challenges he faced as he transitioned into focusing on this particular sport. We explore Aleksinas' early experiences on the basketball court and the dedication and determination he exhibited to improve his skills.

High School Career and Recognition:

Aleksinas' talent and skills on the basketball court began to draw attention during his high school years. We examine his high school career, including his achievements, standout performances, and the recognition he received for his abilities. We delve into the impact of his high school basketball experience on his development as a player and how it shaped his aspirations for the future.

College Recruitment and Decision:

As Aleksinas' high school career progressed, college recruiters took notice of his exceptional abilities. We explore the college recruitment process, the schools that pursued him, and the factors that influenced his decision to choose a particular institution. We delve into the challenges and considerations he faced as he weighed his options and made a significant decision that would shape his collegiate basketball journey.

Athletic and Personal Development:

Beyond the skills and accolades, Aleksinas' early years in sports played a role in his personal development. We examine how athletics influenced his character, work ethic, and discipline. We explore the lessons he learned from sports, including teamwork, perseverance, and resilience, and how these qualities became integral to his success on and off the court.

Conclusion:

In "Towering Above the Rest: Basketball's Elite Big Men," we explore Chuck Aleksinas' early life and athletic pursuits, uncovering the experiences and influences that shaped his passion for sports, particularly basketball. From his upbringing and diverse athletic background to his introduction to basketball and high school career, Aleksinas' journey showcases the foundations of his future success as a professional basketball player. His early years serve as a testament to the importance of nurturing talent and passion in the development of extraordinary athletes.

College and professional career

After an impressive high school basketball career, Chuck Aleksinas took his talents to the collegiate and professional level. In this chapter, we delve into Aleksinas' college and professional career, exploring the challenges he faced, the milestones he achieved, and the impact he made in the world of basketball. From his college recruitment and choice of university to his experiences in the professional leagues, we trace Aleksinas' journey as he pursued his basketball dreams.

College Recruitment and Decision:

After capturing the attention of college recruiters with his exceptional skills and towering stature, Aleksinas faced the decision of where to continue his basketball journey. We explore the recruitment process, the universities that pursued him, and the factors that influenced his final decision. We delve into the expectations and pressures Aleksinas faced as he embarked on his college career and the anticipation surrounding his impact on the collegiate basketball scene.

College Career Highlights:

Once Aleksinas settled into his chosen university, we examine the highlights of his college basketball career. We delve into his individual achievements, notable performances, and contributions to his team's success. From memorable games to conference championships, we paint a picture of Aleksinas' impact on the court and the recognition he garnered during his time in college.

Challenges and Adjustments:

Transitioning from high school to college basketball presented Aleksinas with new challenges and adjustments. We explore the aspects of the college game that tested his skills, including the increased competition, physicality, and tactical demands. We delve into how Aleksinas adapted his game and honed his abilities to thrive at the college level, overcoming obstacles and continuously evolving as a player.

Professional Draft and Path to the NBA:

With a successful college career behind him, Aleksinas set his sights on the professional ranks. We explore his journey through the NBA draft process, the expectations surrounding his selection, and the emotions he experienced on draft day. We delve into the teams that expressed interest in Aleksinas and the factors that influenced his path to the NBA.

Professional Career Milestones:

As Aleksinas embarked on his professional career, we trace his journey through different teams and leagues. We explore the milestones he achieved, such as his NBA debut, memorable performances, and personal accomplishments. From key moments on the court to notable statistics, we paint a comprehensive picture of Aleksinas' professional career and the impact he made in the leagues he competed in.

Overcoming Challenges and Adversity:

Like many professional athletes, Aleksinas faced his share of challenges and adversity throughout his career. We examine the setbacks he encountered, such as injuries, changes in team dynamics, and personal obstacles. We delve into how Aleksinas persevered through these difficulties, showcasing his resilience and determination to overcome obstacles and continue pursuing his passion for basketball.

Legacy and Impact:

Beyond the individual accomplishments, Aleksinas' legacy and impact on the game extend beyond his playing years. We explore the influence he had on future players, the lessons he imparted, and his contributions to the basketball community. We delve into his post-playing career endeavors, including coaching, mentoring, and philanthropy, as he continued to make a positive impact on the sport.

Conclusion:

In "Towering Above the Rest: Basketball's Elite Big Men," we uncover Chuck Aleksinas' college and professional career, tracing his journey from college recruitment to his experiences in the professional leagues. Through challenges, achievements, and contributions, Aleksinas' path showcases the determination and dedication required to succeed at the highest levels of the game. His impact on the basketball community, both on and off the court, solidifies his place among the elite big men of the sport.

After his basketball career came to an end, Chuck Aleksinas ventured into the world beyond the court. In this chapter, we explore Aleksinas' life after basketball, delving into his transition from being a professional athlete to pursuing new endeavors. We examine his post-playing career, business ventures, and the impact he made outside of the basketball world. From his entrepreneurial spirit to his contributions to society, we shed light on the multi-faceted journey of Chuck Aleksinas beyond the confines of the basketball court.

Transitioning from Basketball:

Leaving behind the sport that defined a significant part of his life, Aleksinas faced the challenge of transitioning into a new chapter. We explore the emotions and adjustments he experienced during this period of change. From grappling with the end of a playing career to rediscovering his identity outside of basketball, we delve into the personal journey Aleksinas embarked on as he sought to find purpose and fulfillment in his post-basketball life.

Entrepreneurial Ventures:

With a drive for success and a passion for business, Aleksinas immersed himself in various entrepreneurial ventures. We explore the businesses he established, from ventures related to sports and fitness to other industries. We delve into the challenges and triumphs he encountered as an entrepreneur, showcasing his ability to transfer the skills and discipline honed on the basketball court into the business realm.

Community Involvement and Philanthropy:

Beyond business endeavors, Aleksinas became involved in community initiatives and philanthropy. We examine the causes he championed and the organizations he supported, shedding light on his dedication to making a positive impact on society. Whether through charitable donations, community outreach, or advocacy work, Aleksinas' commitment to giving back serves as an inspiration and showcases his desire to make a difference beyond the realm of sports.

Sports Broadcasting and Media:

Drawing on his knowledge and experience in basketball, Aleksinas ventured into sports broadcasting and media. We explore his foray into commentary, analysis, and sports journalism. From providing expert insights to sharing stories and perspectives from his playing days, we examine Aleksinas' contributions to the media landscape and his ability to stay connected to the sport he loves while engaging with fans and viewers.

Personal Growth and Reflections:

In his life after basketball, Aleksinas embarked on a journey of personal growth and self-reflection. We delve into his pursuit of personal development, including educational pursuits, self-improvement initiatives, and experiences that broadened his horizons beyond the world of sports. Through introspection and introspective interviews, we gain insights into Aleksinas' post-basketball journey and the lessons he learned along the way.

Legacy and Influence:

Aleksinas' legacy extends beyond his playing days. We explore the impact he has had on future generations, both as a basketball player and as a post-basketball figure. We examine the ways in which he has inspired others, whether through his work ethic, resilience, or contributions to society. We delve into the lasting imprint he has made on the basketball community and the broader world, showcasing the depth of his influence and the mark he continues to leave.

Conclusion:

In "Towering Above the Rest: Basketball's Elite Big Men," we uncover Chuck Aleksinas' life after basketball and his ventures beyond the court. From entrepreneurial pursuits to community involvement, Aleksinas' post-playing journey showcases his versatility, determination, and commitment to making a positive impact. His ability to adapt, grow, and thrive in various fields beyond basketball solidifies his legacy as an influential figure both within and outside the realm of sports.

Reflections on being a tall player

In this chapter, we delve into Chuck Aleksinas' reflections on his experience as a tall player in the world of basketball. Standing at an impressive 7 feet tall, Aleksinas encountered unique challenges, opportunities, and perceptions throughout his career. We explore his thoughts, insights, and personal anecdotes, shedding light on the intricacies of being a towering presence on the court. From the physical advantages to the societal expectations, we uncover Aleksinas' perspective on what it means to navigate the basketball world as a tall player.

Embracing Height and Identity:

Aleksinas reflects on how his height shaped his identity as a basketball player and as an individual. We delve into his journey of self-acceptance, exploring the ways in which he embraced his stature and harnessed it to his advantage on the court. We examine the physical attributes and skills that accompany being a tall player, and how Aleksinas harnessed these traits to become a dominant force in the game.

Challenges and Stereotypes:

Being a tall player also presented Aleksinas with a unique set of challenges and stereotypes. We explore the misconceptions and expectations he encountered, both from opponents and from society at large. From assumptions about his athletic abilities to the limitations placed on tall players, we delve into Aleksinas' experiences and how he overcame or defied these stereotypes to forge his own path in the game.

Physicality and Conditioning:

The physical demands of being a tall player in basketball cannot be overlooked. Aleksinas reflects on the unique challenges he faced in terms of conditioning, injury prevention, and physical matchups. We delve into his training regimen, diet, and dedication to maintaining peak physical condition. We also explore the toll that the physicality of the game took on his body and how he managed to stay resilient throughout his career.

Mental and Psychological Factors:

Height can also have significant psychological effects on players. Aleksinas shares his insights into the mental aspects of the game, including the pressure to perform, the expectations placed on tall players, and the mental fortitude required to navigate these challenges. We examine his strategies for staying focused, dealing with criticism, and maintaining confidence despite the unique psychological pressures he faced.

Teammates, Coaches, and Support Systems:

Throughout his career, Aleksinas relied on the support of teammates, coaches, and support staff to navigate the challenges of being a tall player. We explore the dynamics of his relationships within teams, the role of coaches in harnessing his potential, and the support systems that helped him overcome obstacles. We also delve into the camaraderie and unique bond that forms among players, especially within the context of being a tall player.

Off-Court Experiences and Public Perception:

Beyond the basketball court, Aleksinas reflects on how his height influenced public perception and his interactions with fans and the media. We explore the attention he received as a tall player and the ways in which he managed his public image. We delve into the experiences, both positive and negative, that shaped his understanding of how society views and treats tall athletes.

Legacy and Inspiring Future Generations:

As Aleksinas reflects on his career as a tall player, we examine the legacy he hopes to leave behind. We explore the impact he wishes to have on future generations of tall players, the lessons he wants to impart, and the inspiration he hopes to provide. We delve into his post-playing career endeavors, including mentoring and coaching, as avenues through which he continues to shape the experiences of tall athletes in the game.

Conclusion:

In "Towering Above the Rest: Basketball's Elite Big Men," we uncover Chuck Aleksinas' reflections on being a tall player in the world of basketball. Through his personal insights, we gain a deeper understanding of the complexities and nuances of navigating the game as a towering presence. Aleksinas' experiences and reflections serve as a testament to the unique challenges, advantages, and responsibilities that come with being a tall player, leaving a lasting impact on the basketball community and inspiring future generations to embrace their own heights, both literally and metaphorically.

Chapter 5: Dave Newmark - 7'0" – 1972

Newmark's early years and interest in basketball

In this chapter, we delve into the early years of Dave Newmark, a towering figure standing at 7 feet tall, and his deep-rooted interest in the game of basketball. We explore the factors that ignited his passion for the sport, his journey through adolescence, and the formative experiences that shaped his basketball aspirations. From his early encounters with the game to his development as a young athlete, we uncover the foundational elements that set the stage for Newmark's remarkable basketball career.

Childhood Influences and Introduction to Basketball:

We begin by examining the influences in Newmark's childhood that sparked his interest in basketball. Whether it was watching games on television, attending local basketball events, or having family members involved in the sport, we explore the pivotal moments and individuals that captured his attention and ignited his love for the game. We delve into the early experiences that nurtured his passion and set him on the path to becoming a professional basketball player.

Growth Spurt and Physical Transformation:

One defining aspect of Newmark's journey was a significant growth spurt that propelled him to a towering height. We explore the physical changes he underwent during this period and the impact it had on his basketball aspirations. From adjusting to his rapidly changing body to harnessing the advantages of his height, we delve into how Newmark navigated these physical transformations and discovered his unique potential on the basketball court.

High School Years and Skill Development:

During his high school years, Newmark honed his basketball skills and began making a name for himself on the local basketball scene. We delve into his experiences playing for his high school team, the challenges he faced as a tall player, and the ways in which he worked to improve his game. From developing fundamental skills to refining his understanding of the sport, we explore the dedication and hard work that laid the foundation for his future success.

College Recruitment and Decision-Making Process:

As Newmark's skills continued to develop, he attracted attention from college basketball programs across the country. We explore the recruitment process, the schools that showed interest in him, and the factors that influenced his decision. From considering academic opportunities to evaluating basketball programs and coaching staff, we delve into the pivotal moments and considerations that shaped Newmark's college choice and set the stage for his collegiate basketball career.

College Career at Illinois State:

Newmark's college career at Illinois State University played a significant role in shaping his basketball journey. We delve into his experiences playing for the Redbirds, his contributions to the team, and the highlights of his collegiate career. From memorable games to individual achievements, we explore how Newmark's time at Illinois State helped him further develop as a player and prepared him for the professional level.

Challenges and Growth:

Throughout his early years, Newmark undoubtedly faced challenges as a tall player. We examine the obstacles he encountered, both on and off the court, and how he overcame them. Whether it was adapting to different playing styles, dealing with increased expectations, or managing the physical demands of the game, we delve into Newmark's resilience and determination in the face of adversity.

Passion for the Game and Personal Growth:

Beyond the technical aspects of basketball, Newmark's journey also encompassed personal growth and a deepening love for the game. We explore the ways in which his passion for basketball continued to evolve, driving him to push boundaries, improve his skills, and contribute to the teams he played for. We also delve into the mentors, coaches, and teammates who played a pivotal role in shaping his basketball journey and fostering his love for the game.

Conclusion:

In "Towering Above the Rest: Basketball's Elite Big Men," we uncover the early years and formative experiences of Dave Newmark, a 7-foot tall player who made his mark on the basketball world. From his childhood influences to his high school and college career, we gain insights into the foundations of his basketball journey and the deep-rooted interest that propelled him toward success. As we explore Newmark's early years and interest in basketball, we set the stage for the subsequent chapters, where we delve further into his professional career, challenges faced, and lasting impact on the game.

College career at Illinois State

In this chapter, we delve into Dave Newmark's college career at Illinois State University, a pivotal period that played a significant role in shaping his basketball journey. We explore the challenges, triumphs, and growth he experienced during his time as a Redbird. From his initial transition to college basketball to his contributions to the team's success, we uncover the memorable moments and defining aspects of Newmark's college career.

Transitioning to College Basketball:

Newmark's transition from high school to college basketball marked a significant step in his basketball journey. We explore the adjustments he had to make both on and off the court, including the higher level of competition, the increased demands of college athletics, and the balancing act of academics and sports. We delve into the challenges he faced during this transitional phase and how he navigated them to find his footing within the college basketball landscape.

Joining the Illinois State Redbirds:

At Illinois State University, Newmark became a key member of the Redbirds basketball program. We explore the recruitment process that led him to Illinois State, the coaches and teammates who welcomed him into the program, and the role he played within the team. From his first practices to his early games as a Redbird, we uncover the initial impressions he made and the expectations that were placed on his broad shoulders.

Development as a Player:

During his college years, Newmark underwent significant growth and development as a basketball player. We delve into the specific areas of his game that he focused on improving, such as his post moves, shooting range, defensive presence, and overall basketball IQ. We examine the coaching strategies and training regimens that helped shape his skills and the ways in which he applied those skills on the court to make an impact for the Redbirds.

Individual Achievements and Accolades:

As Newmark's college career progressed, he began to receive recognition for his exceptional play and contributions to the team. We explore the individual achievements and accolades he earned, such as conference honors, All-American nominations, and any school records he set during his time at Illinois State. We delve into the moments that defined his college career and solidified his reputation as a formidable force in college basketball.

Team Success and Memorable Games:

While individual accomplishments are noteworthy, Newmark's impact extended beyond his personal achievements. We highlight the team successes he experienced during his college career, including conference championships, postseason appearances, and memorable games that showcased his skills and leadership. Whether it was a hard-fought victory against a rival team or a deep playoff run, we delve into the collective moments that elevated the Redbirds' success and the role Newmark played in those achievements.

Off-Court Influence and Leadership:

Newmark's influence extended beyond the basketball court. We explore his role as a leader within the team, the respect he garnered from his coaches and teammates, and the ways in which he positively impacted the program's culture. From his work ethic and dedication to his supportive nature and mentorship, we delve into the intangible qualities that made Newmark a valued presence both on and off the court.

Conclusion:

As we conclude the exploration of Dave Newmark's college career at Illinois State, we reflect on the transformative experiences, challenges overcome, and successes achieved. His time as a Redbird laid the groundwork for his future endeavors in professional basketball and left an indelible mark on the program and the basketball community. From his individual achievements to the collective accomplishments of the team, Newmark's college career serves as a testament to his talent, hard work, and unwavering commitment to the game.

Professional career and challenges faced

In this chapter, we explore Dave Newmark's professional basketball career and the challenges he faced as he transitioned from the college ranks to the world of professional basketball. We delve into the different teams he played for, the adjustments he had to make, and the obstacles he encountered along the way. From his rookie season to the culmination of his professional journey, we uncover the highs and lows, the triumphs and setbacks that defined Newmark's professional career.

Entering the Professional Ranks:

After a successful college career at Illinois State University, Newmark set his sights on the professional ranks. We delve into the process of entering the NBA and the different opportunities that awaited him. Whether it was being drafted, signing as a free agent, or exploring international basketball options, we explore the path Newmark took and the decisions that shaped the beginning of his professional journey.

Adapting to the NBA:

Transitioning to the NBA presented Newmark with new challenges and a higher level of competition. We examine the adjustments he had to make to his game, the style of play he encountered, and the strategies he employed to adapt to the demands of the professional league. From refining his skills to understanding the nuances of the NBA game, we delve into the steps Newmark took to establish himself in the league.

Team Dynamics and Roles:

Throughout his professional career, Newmark played for multiple teams, each with its own unique dynamics and expectations. We explore the different environments he found himself in, the teammates he played alongside, and the roles he was assigned within each team. We delve into the challenges of fitting into different systems, building chemistry with new teammates, and fulfilling the specific responsibilities that came with each team and coaching staff.

Injuries and Setbacks:

No professional career is without its share of challenges, and Newmark faced his fair share of setbacks. We examine the injuries he encountered and the impact they had on his playing time and overall career trajectory. From the physical rehabilitation to the mental resilience required to bounce back, we delve into the obstacles he faced and the determination he demonstrated in overcoming them.

Professional Milestones and Achievements:

Amidst the challenges, Newmark also achieved significant milestones in his professional career. We highlight the standout performances, individual accolades, and team accomplishments that marked his journey. Whether it was setting career-highs, being selected for All-Star games, or contributing to playoff runs, we delve into the moments that showcased his skill and made an impact on the basketball community.

International Basketball Ventures:

In addition to his NBA career, Newmark may have explored opportunities in international basketball. We examine any ventures he pursued overseas, the leagues he played in, and the experiences he gained from competing on the global stage. We explore how these international experiences broadened his perspective of the game and influenced his development as a player.

The End of a Professional Career:

Like all professional journeys, Newmark's career eventually came to a close. We explore the factors that led to his retirement, whether it was due to age, injuries, or personal decisions. We delve into the emotions and reflections that accompanied the end of his playing days and the transition to a new phase of life.

Legacy and Impact:

As we conclude the chapter, we reflect on Dave Newmark's professional career and the lasting impact he left on the game. We examine his influence beyond the court, such as his contributions to the community, his mentorship of younger players, and the ways in which he continued to contribute to the sport even after his playing career. We celebrate his achievements and the legacy he established in the world of professional basketball.

Conclusion:

Dave Newmark's professional career was a journey of highs and lows, triumphs and challenges. From the transition to the NBA to the obstacles faced and the achievements attained, his story serves as a testament to the resilience and perseverance required to succeed in the competitive world of professional basketball. Newmark's career exemplifies the dedication and passion that fuel athletes, and his experiences provide valuable insights into the realities of a professional basketball career.

In this chapter, we explore the lasting legacy and impact of Dave Newmark on the game of basketball. Beyond his individual accomplishments and contributions, we delve into the broader influence he had on the sport, both during his playing days and in the years that followed. From his on-court prowess to his off-court endeavors, we examine how Newmark's presence left a lasting imprint on the basketball community.

Setting New Standards:

Dave Newmark's career redefined expectations for players of his stature. Standing at 7 feet tall, he showcased the versatility and skill set that big men could possess. We examine how his unique abilities as a tall player challenged conventional norms and expanded the possibilities for players of similar size. His success and impact served as an inspiration for future generations of tall athletes, opening doors and encouraging them to explore their full potential.

Influence on Playing Style:

Newmark's playing style and skill set influenced the way the game was played. We analyze his strengths and how they translated into his impact on the court. Whether it was his scoring ability, defensive presence, or court vision, we explore how his skills reshaped strategies and game plans.

Coaches and teams had to adapt to counter his dominance, leading to new approaches in defending and utilizing tall players.

Role Model for Tall Players:

As one of the notable tall players of his era, Newmark became a role model for aspiring athletes who shared his height. We examine how his achievements and demeanor served as an inspiration for other tall players who sought to make their mark in basketball. From his work ethic to his professionalism, Newmark's character set a positive example for those looking to navigate the unique challenges and opportunities that come with being a tall athlete.

Impact on Team Dynamics:

Newmark's presence on the court had a significant impact on team dynamics. We delve into how his size and skills influenced the strategies and game plans of opposing teams. The need to account for Newmark's abilities in both offense and defense often led to adjustments in rotations, defensive schemes, and overall team strategy. We explore how his presence affected the dynamics and gameplay of the teams he played for and against.

Community Engagement and Philanthropy:

Beyond his on-court contributions, Newmark's impact extended to the communities he was a part of. We examine his involvement in charitable endeavors and community outreach programs. From basketball clinics for youth to contributions to charitable organizations, we explore how Newmark used his platform to give back and make a positive difference in the lives of others. His commitment to community engagement serves as a testament to the power of athletes to effect change beyond the confines of the basketball court.

Mentorship and Player Development:

Throughout his career and even in his post-playing days, Newmark served as a mentor to young players. We highlight his dedication to nurturing and developing talent, whether through formal coaching roles or informal guidance. His willingness to share his knowledge and experiences with the next generation of players had a profound impact on their development, contributing to the growth and success of future basketball stars.

Influence on Basketball Culture:

Newmark's impact transcended the court and permeated basketball culture. We explore how his style of play, accomplishments, and persona influenced the perception and appreciation of tall players in the basketball community. Whether through media coverage, fan support, or the recognition of his contributions, Newmark's legacy played a role in shaping the broader narrative surrounding tall players in the game.

Recognition and Honors:

We delve into the recognition and honors bestowed upon Newmark throughout his career and beyond. Whether it was All-Star selections, awards, or inductions into Hall of Fame, we examine how his accomplishments were celebrated and acknowledged by the basketball community. We explore the significance of these accolades in cementing his legacy and affirming his impact on the game.

Conclusion:

Dave Newmark's legacy and impact on the game of basketball are far-reaching. From his on-court achievements to his contributions off the court, his influence extended beyond the years he played. We reflect on the lasting imprint he left on the sport, the doors he opened for tall players, and the inspiration he provided for future generations. Newmark's legacy serves as a testament to the transformative power of athletes and their ability to shape the game they love.

Chapter 6: Stuart Gray - 7'1" – 1989

Gray's upbringing and basketball journey

In this chapter, we delve into the upbringing and basketball journey of Stuart Gray, a towering figure in the world of basketball. We explore the early influences, challenges, and experiences that shaped Gray's path to becoming a professional athlete. From his formative years to his emergence as a basketball standout, we unravel the factors that contributed to his development and set the stage for his remarkable career.

Family and Early Life:

We begin by examining Gray's family background and early life. We explore the values instilled in him by his parents and the role they played in nurturing his love for the game. We delve into his childhood experiences, including his early encounters with basketball, and how these formative years laid the foundation for his future success.

Growing Pains and Physical Development:

Gray's remarkable height played a pivotal role in his basketball journey. We explore the challenges and adjustments he faced as he experienced rapid physical growth during his teenage years. From the physical demands on his body to the psychological adjustments required to navigate daily life, we analyze the impact of his towering stature on his personal development and basketball aspirations.

High School Career and Recognition:

Gray's talent on the basketball court began to shine during his high school years. We explore his high school career, analyzing his skills, performances, and the recognition he garnered as a rising star. From standout moments to team successes, we highlight the milestones that propelled him onto the radar of college recruiters and basketball enthusiasts alike.

College Recruitment and Decision:

The college recruitment process is a pivotal moment for any aspiring athlete, and Gray's journey was no exception. We delve into the offers, considerations, and ultimately, the decision-making process that led him to choose his collegiate destination. We examine the factors that influenced his choice and the impact it had on his basketball career trajectory.

College Career and Achievements:

Gray's collegiate years were marked by notable achievements and contributions to his team. We explore his time on the college basketball court, analyzing his skills, statistics, and impact on the game. From memorable performances to team successes, we highlight the key moments that solidified his reputation as a formidable player and caught the attention of professional scouts.

Overcoming Challenges:

No basketball journey is without its share of challenges, and Gray's path was no different. We explore the obstacles he encountered throughout his basketball career, from injuries and setbacks to the pressures of expectations and competition. We delve into his resilience and determination in overcoming these challenges and how they ultimately shaped his character and resilience both on and off the court.

Personal Growth and Maturation:

Beyond the basketball court, Gray's journey also encompassed personal growth and maturation. We examine how his experiences as a college athlete and the responsibilities that came with it contributed to his overall development as a person. From time management to leadership skills, we analyze the lessons he learned and the growth he experienced during this transformative period.

Conclusion:

Stuart Gray's upbringing and basketball journey are a testament to the influence of early experiences, perseverance, and personal growth in shaping a player's career. From his formative years to his college accomplishments, his path to success was paved with challenges and triumphs. Gray's story serves as inspiration for aspiring athletes, highlighting the importance of resilience, dedication, and a strong support system in achieving one's goals.

In this chapter, we delve into Stuart Gray's college career at UCLA, where he left an indelible mark on the basketball program and established himself as one of the premier big men of his era. We explore his journey from being a highly recruited prospect to his stellar performances on the court. From his early days at UCLA to his achievements and impact on the team, we unravel the key moments and experiences that defined Gray's college career.

Choosing UCLA:

We begin by examining the factors that led Stuart Gray to choose UCLA as his collegiate destination. We delve into the recruiting process, the allure of the UCLA basketball program, and the influence of coaches, teammates, and the university's rich basketball history on his decision. We explore how UCLA's prestigious basketball legacy and its emphasis on player development aligned with Gray's aspirations and contributed to his overall growth as a player.

Freshman Year and Adjustments:

Gray's freshman year at UCLA was a period of adjustment, both on and off the court. We explore his transition from high school to college basketball, the challenges he faced, and the adjustments he had to make to adapt to the increased level of competition and the demands of being a student-athlete. We analyze his performance during his first collegiate season, highlighting the glimpses of potential and the areas where he showed room for growth.

Skill Development and Coaching:

Under the guidance of renowned UCLA coach, John Wooden, Gray's skills and basketball IQ underwent significant development during his college years. We delve into the coaching strategies employed by Wooden and the UCLA coaching staff, the individualized attention Gray received, and the emphasis on fundamental skills that shaped his game. We explore how Gray's work ethic and dedication to improvement translated into tangible on-court results.

On-Court Dominance:

As Gray progressed through his college career, his impact on the court became increasingly evident. We analyze his statistics, performances, and contributions to the team's success. From dominant post play to rebounding prowess, we highlight Gray's strengths and the strategies employed by opponents to contain him. We delve into memorable games and moments where Gray's presence was pivotal in securing victories and advancing the team's aspirations.

Team Success and Championships:

Gray's college career was not only marked by individual accomplishments but also by team success. We delve into the NCAA Tournament runs and the championships that Gray and his UCLA teammates achieved. We analyze the chemistry and dynamics of the teams, the role Gray played in the team's success, and the strategies employed by opponents to counter his impact. We examine the lasting legacy of those championship teams and their place in UCLA basketball history.

Off-Court Influence and Leadership:

Beyond his on-court performances, Gray's impact extended to his leadership and influence off the court. We explore his role as a team leader, the respect he commanded from his teammates, and the ways in which he contributed to the overall culture and camaraderie of the UCLA basketball program. We analyze his involvement in community initiatives, his academic achievements, and the lasting impression he left on his teammates and coaches.

Legacy and Impact:

Gray's college career at UCLA left an enduring legacy that continues to resonate to this day. We reflect on his impact on the UCLA basketball program, the lessons learned from his success, and his influence on future generations of players. We explore how his accomplishments and leadership helped shape the perception of UCLA as a basketball powerhouse and influenced the recruitment of future talented athletes to the program.

Conclusion:

Stuart Gray's college career at UCLA was a transformative period marked by individual growth, team success, and a lasting legacy. From his freshman year adjustments to his dominant performances and championships, Gray's impact on the court was undeniable. His leadership, skill development, and contributions to the UCLA basketball program solidified his place among the greats. Gray's college career serves as a testament to the transformative power of collegiate athletics and the enduring impact a player can have on a program's history.

Professional career and achievements

In this chapter, we delve into Stuart Gray's professional basketball career after his successful college tenure at UCLA. We explore his journey from being a highly regarded prospect to his experiences in various professional leagues. From his initial steps into the NBA to his achievements and challenges faced along the way, we unravel the key moments and milestones that shaped Gray's professional career.

Draft and NBA Beginnings:

We begin by examining Stuart Gray's entry into the NBA through the draft process. We explore the anticipation and excitement surrounding his selection, the team that acquired his rights, and the expectations placed upon him as a highly touted prospect. We delve into his early experiences in training camp, preseason games, and his first regular-season appearances in the NBA, analyzing his initial performances and the adjustments he had to make to adapt to the professional level.

NBA Career and Team Contributions:

Gray's NBA career spanned several teams, and we delve into each chapter of his professional journey. We explore the teams he played for, his roles within those organizations, and his contributions to their success. From his early seasons as a role player to potentially becoming a starter, we analyze his statistics, playing style, and the impact he had on the court. We highlight standout performances, memorable games, and the recognition he received for his contributions.

Challenges and Setbacks:

Like many professional athletes, Gray faced his fair share of challenges and setbacks throughout his career. We explore the injuries, obstacles, and adversity he encountered, and how he overcame or navigated through them. We delve into the mental and physical toll of injuries, the impact they had on his playing time and performance, and the resilience he displayed in bouncing back. We also examine any off-court challenges or personal circumstances that influenced his professional journey.

International Stints and Global Exposure:

Beyond the NBA, Gray's professional career may have taken him to various international leagues. We explore his experiences playing overseas and the opportunities that arose from these stints. We analyze the impact of playing in different basketball cultures, the adjustments required, and the exposure he gained on the global stage. We highlight any notable achievements or recognition received during his international career.

Achievements and Individual Accolades:

Throughout his professional career, Gray achieved significant milestones and garnered individual accolades. We delve into his statistical achievements, such as career highs, rebounds, blocks, and any records he set or approached. We also explore any honors or awards he received, such as All-Star selections, All-League recognition, or inclusion in various basketball rankings. We analyze the significance of these achievements and their reflection of Gray's contributions to the game.

Contributions Beyond the Court:

Gray's impact extended beyond his on-court performances. We explore any community involvement, philanthropic efforts, or leadership roles he took on during his professional career. We highlight his contributions to the basketball community, the positive influence he had on aspiring players, and any mentorship or coaching endeavors he pursued. We examine the lasting legacy of his off-court contributions and the impact he made in the lives of others.

Retirement and Life After Basketball:

As Gray's professional career eventually came to a close, we delve into his transition into retirement and his pursuits outside of basketball. We explore his post-basketball endeavors, such as business ventures, coaching roles, or involvement in the basketball industry. We examine how Gray's experiences as a professional player shaped his post-playing career and the lessons he carried forward from his time in the game.

Conclusion:

Stuart Gray's professional career was marked by his contributions to the NBA, international leagues, and the basketball community as a whole. From his early days in the NBA to his achievements, challenges, and global exposure, Gray's journey offers insights into the competitive world of professional basketball. His impact on the court, his resilience in the face of adversity, and his contributions beyond the game serve as a testament to his enduring legacy.

Life after basketball and current pursuits

In this chapter, we explore Stuart Gray's life after his professional basketball career and delve into his current pursuits. Transitioning from the competitive world of basketball to the next phase of life can be challenging for many athletes, and we examine how Gray navigated this transition and found new avenues for personal and professional growth. From his post-basketball endeavors to his current passions and contributions, we shed light on the remarkable journey of Stuart Gray beyond the court.

Retirement and Reflections:

We begin by exploring Gray's retirement from professional basketball and the initial period of adjustment he faced. Retirement can bring a mix of emotions, and we delve into Gray's reflections on his basketball career, the impact the game had on his life, and the lessons he learned along the way. We examine how he processed the transition and the insights he gained about personal identity, purpose, and life beyond the sport.

Business Ventures and Entrepreneurship:

One aspect of Gray's life after basketball is his foray into business ventures and entrepreneurship. We delve into the specific ventures he pursued, whether it be starting his own company, investing in existing businesses, or engaging in entrepreneurial endeavors. We explore the industries he entered, the challenges he encountered, and the successes he achieved. We examine how Gray's experiences as a professional athlete translated into the business world and shaped his approach to entrepreneurship.

Coaching and Mentorship:

Gray's passion for basketball didn't end with his retirement as a player. We delve into his involvement in coaching and mentorship roles, exploring how he shared his knowledge and experience with aspiring athletes. We examine the teams or organizations he worked with, the impact he made on young players' development, and the satisfaction he derived from nurturing talent and helping others succeed. We highlight any notable coaching achievements or mentoring relationships he formed.

Basketball Community Involvement:

Beyond coaching, Gray's commitment to the basketball community may have extended to other forms of involvement. We explore his contributions as an ambassador for the sport, such as participation in youth basketball programs, charitable initiatives, or basketball-related events and clinics. We delve into his efforts to give back to the game that shaped his life and the ways he made a positive impact on the basketball community at large.

Personal Growth and Development:

Retirement often provides an opportunity for personal growth and self-discovery. We delve into Gray's personal journey after basketball, exploring any pursuits he undertook to enhance his skills, knowledge, or well-being. This may include further education, personal development programs, or involvement in hobbies and interests outside of basketball. We examine how Gray continued to evolve as an individual and expand his horizons beyond the confines of his basketball career.

Philanthropy and Community Service:

Gray's post-basketball life may have also involved philanthropic endeavors and community service. We explore any causes or organizations he supported, the impact he made through his philanthropic efforts, and the ways he gave back to his community. We examine the issues or initiatives that resonated with Gray and how he used his platform and resources to make a positive difference in the lives of others.

Current Passions and Pursuits:

Lastly, we explore Gray's current passions and pursuits. Whether it be new interests, hobbies, or areas of focus, we delve into the aspects of his life that bring him joy, fulfillment, and purpose. This may include involvement in non-profit organizations, creative endeavors, personal projects, or even a return to the basketball world in a different capacity. We examine how Gray continues to shape his post-basketball life and find fulfillment in new endeavors.

Conclusion:

Stuart Gray's life after basketball is a testament to his resilience, adaptability, and passion for growth. From entrepreneurship to coaching, community involvement to personal development, Gray's journey showcases the possibilities that exist beyond the confines of a professional sports career. His continued impact on the basketball community and his pursuit of new passions serve as an inspiration for athletes and individuals alike.

Conclusion

The common threads among tall players

As we conclude our exploration of NBA players who were exactly 7 feet or taller and retired before 1990, it becomes evident that there are common threads that unite these towering athletes. Despite their individual stories and experiences, certain themes emerge that highlight the unique challenges and profound impact of being exceptionally tall in the world of basketball. In this concluding section, we delve into these common threads, shedding light on the shared experiences and legacies of these remarkable big men.

Physical Advantages and Challenges:

One of the primary common threads among tall players is the physical advantages and challenges they face. We delve into the inherent advantages of height on the basketball court, such as rebounding, shot-blocking, and altering opponents' shots. We discuss the challenges that come with being exceptionally tall, including coordination, agility, and the strain on the body. By examining these physical aspects, we gain a deeper understanding of how height influences a player's style of play and career trajectory.

Impact on the Game:

Another significant common thread is the profound impact that these giants have had on the game of basketball. We analyze how their presence on the court has shaped the strategies and dynamics of the sport. From dominating the paint to altering offensive schemes, these tall players have left an indelible mark on the game's history. We explore the ways in which their presence has influenced team strategies, defensive systems, and the evolution of the game itself.

Trailblazers and Pioneers:

Many of the tall players discussed in this book can be considered trailblazers and pioneers in their own right. We highlight the ways in which they paved the way for future generations of big men. Whether it be breaking barriers, setting records, or challenging conventional wisdom, these players left a lasting impact on the perception and treatment of tall athletes in the basketball world. We examine their contributions to changing stereotypes, expanding opportunities, and inspiring others to reach new heights.

Overcoming Adversity:

While height can bring inherent advantages, it also presents its own set of challenges. A common thread among these tall players is the adversity they faced throughout their careers. From injuries and setbacks to the pressure of expectations, they navigated obstacles that tested their resilience and determination. We explore the ways in which these athletes overcame adversity, demonstrating the mental fortitude and perseverance required to excel at the highest level of the game.

Legacy and Influence:

The final common thread we examine is the enduring legacy and influence of these tall players. We reflect on their impact beyond their playing careers, assessing how their contributions have shaped the basketball landscape. From inspiring future generations to redefining positions and reimagining what is possible for tall players, their influence extends far beyond their individual accomplishments. We analyze their post-retirement endeavors, whether it be coaching, mentoring, or involvement in the basketball community, and how they continue to make a lasting impact on the game.

Lessons and Inspirations:

Throughout this book, we have explored the stories of lesser-known tall players who retired before 1990, uncovering their journeys, triumphs, and challenges. In this concluding section, we distill the lessons and inspirations gleaned from their experiences. We discuss the perseverance, passion, and resilience exhibited by these athletes and how their stories can serve as motivation for aspiring basketball players, regardless of their height or background.

Final Thoughts:

"Towering Above the Rest: Basketball's Elite Big Men" has provided a window into the lives of NBA players who stood tall on the court. Through their stories, we have gained insights into the fascination with height in basketball, the impact of giants on the game, and the often-overlooked narratives of lesser-known tall players. As we conclude, we recognize the collective experiences and legacies that bind these athletes together and appreciate the enduring contributions they have made to the sport we love. Their stories will continue to inspire and captivate basketball fans for generations to come.

In the realm of basketball, giants—players who stand at least 7 feet tall—occupy a unique position. While their height grants them inherent advantages on the court, it also presents a distinct set of challenges that shape their careers and personal experiences. In this concluding section, we delve into the unique challenges faced by these towering athletes. By examining the physical, psychological, and societal aspects, we gain a deeper understanding of the complexities of being a giant in the basketball world.

Physical Challenges:

One of the most apparent challenges faced by giants is the physical toll that their height places on their bodies. We explore the strain on their joints, the increased risk of injuries, and the demands of maintaining their athleticism. From back problems to foot issues, these players often encounter unique health challenges that require careful management and specialized training. We discuss the importance of proper conditioning and the physical sacrifices they make to excel in their sport.

Coordination and Agility:

While height can be an advantage, it also presents challenges in terms of coordination and agility. We examine how giants must adapt their movements and footwork to navigate the court effectively. The elongated limbs and larger frames can pose difficulties in terms of balance, agility, and fluidity of motion. We explore the training and techniques employed to enhance coordination and ensure that their size does not impede their overall performance.

Expectations and Pressure:

Another significant challenge faced by giants is the weight of expectations placed upon them. We discuss the pressure to live up to the potential associated with their height, the scrutiny from fans and media, and the burden of being seen as dominant forces on the court. These players often face heightened expectations to deliver consistent performances, which can lead to added stress and mental strain. We examine the psychological impact of such expectations and how giants navigate the mental challenges of the game.

Social and Cultural Perceptions:

Giants in basketball also contend with social and cultural perceptions surrounding their height. We delve into the stereotypes and assumptions associated with tall individuals, including the perception of being physically dominant or lacking coordination. We examine how these preconceived notions can influence how giants are viewed and treated both on and off the court. Additionally, we discuss the challenges of finding clothes, furniture, and everyday objects that accommodate their stature, highlighting the practical implications of their height in daily life.

Balancing Identity and Individuality:

Being a giant in basketball often means grappling with the balance between identity and individuality. We explore how these players navigate the public's perception of them primarily based on their height, while also striving to be recognized for their skills, achievements, and unique personalities. We discuss their efforts to establish their individual identities beyond their physical stature and the importance of self-expression in an industry that often focuses on physical attributes.

Relationships and Lifestyle:

The unique challenges faced by giants extend beyond the court into their personal lives. We explore the impact of height on relationships, both romantic and platonic, and the challenges of finding partners and friends who can relate to their experiences. We discuss the logistical challenges of travel, accommodations, and everyday activities that giants must navigate. We also examine the lifestyle adjustments required to accommodate their physical needs and maintain a balanced and fulfilling life.

Support Systems and Resilience:

Despite the challenges they face, giants in basketball often develop strong support systems to help them navigate their careers. We discuss the importance of coaches, teammates, and family in providing emotional support, guidance, and mentorship. We explore the resilience exhibited by these players in overcoming setbacks and how they draw on their support networks to persevere through adversity. We highlight the personal growth and character development that can result from the challenges faced by giants.

Conclusion:

The challenges faced by giants in basketball are multi-faceted and nuanced, ranging from physical and psychological demands to societal expectations and cultural perceptions. Throughout this book, we have explored the stories of towering athletes who have faced these challenges head-on, showcasing their resilience, determination, and unwavering passion for the game. By understanding and appreciating the unique struggles they encounter, we gain a greater appreciation for their contributions to the sport and the impact they have on and off the court. The stories of these giants serve as a reminder that true greatness goes beyond physical stature, and their legacies will continue to inspire future generations of basketball players and fans alike.

Reflections on the impact of giants on the game

Throughout this book, we have delved into the lives and careers of towering athletes who stood at least 7 feet tall, examining their journeys, challenges, and contributions to the game of basketball. In this concluding section, we reflect on the profound impact that these giants have had on the sport, both on and off the court. From their dominant presence in the paint to their enduring legacies, their influence reverberates through the history of basketball.

Revolutionizing the Game:

One cannot discuss the impact of giants without acknowledging the revolution they brought to the game of basketball. We explore how their height and physical dominance have transformed the dynamics of the sport. From dominating the rebounding game to altering defensive strategies, giants have forced teams to adapt their playing styles and develop innovative approaches to counter their influence. We discuss how their presence has reshaped the strategies, tactics, and overall gameplay in basketball.

Dominance in the Paint:

One of the most significant contributions of giants to the game is their dominant presence in the paint. We delve into their impact on shot-blocking, rim protection, and altering opponents' shots. We analyze the defensive prowess of these towering athletes, their ability to intimidate opponents, and their role as defensive anchors for their teams. We also discuss their offensive contributions, including scoring in the post, finishing at the rim, and the challenges they pose for opposing defenses.

Changing Team Dynamics:

Giants have a profound influence on team dynamics, both on and off the court. We examine how their presence affects roster construction, lineup strategies, and overall team chemistry. We explore the importance of finding the right balance between utilizing their unique skills and integrating them effectively into team systems. Additionally, we discuss the symbiotic relationship between giants and their teammates, highlighting the importance of teamwork and the interplay between different positions on the court.

Inspiration and Aspirations:

The impact of giants extends beyond their on-court performance. We reflect on how their towering presence inspires aspiring basketball players, particularly those who possess exceptional height. We discuss the role models they become and the dreams they ignite in young athletes who aspire to reach similar heights. We examine the impact of their success on grassroots basketball programs, coaching approaches, and player development, as well as their influence in nurturing the next generation of giants in the game.

Community Engagement and Philanthropy:

Many giants in basketball have used their platform to make a positive impact off the court. We highlight their involvement in community outreach programs, philanthropic endeavors, and charitable initiatives. We discuss how they leverage their influence to effect change, support underprivileged communities, and promote social causes. From establishing foundations to organizing basketball clinics, these giants serve as ambassadors for the game and make meaningful contributions beyond their basketball careers.

Media and Pop Culture:

The impact of giants in basketball extends into the realm of media and popular culture. We examine how their larger-than-life personas, remarkable skills, and captivating narratives have captured the attention of fans worldwide. We discuss their representation in films, documentaries, and advertisements, as well as their role in shaping basketball's image and global appeal. We also explore the influence of social media in amplifying their voices and connecting with fans on a more personal level.

Legacy and Lasting Impact:

As we conclude our exploration of giants in basketball, we reflect on their enduring legacy and lasting impact on the sport. We discuss the records they set, the championships they won, and the milestones they achieved. We also highlight their contributions to the growth and global expansion of basketball, and how they continue to be celebrated as icons of the game. Their influence transcends generations, and their names are etched in the annals of basketball history.

Conclusion:

The impact of giants on the game of basketball is immeasurable. From revolutionizing playing styles to inspiring future generations, their influence stretches far beyond their towering presence on the court. As we reflect on their contributions, we recognize the unique challenges they face, the admiration they evoke, and the lasting legacy they leave behind. These giants have left an indelible mark on the sport, shaping the way we perceive and appreciate basketball. Their impact will continue to resonate in the hearts of fans and the minds of players for years to come.

THE END

Key Terms and Definitions

To help you better understand the language and concepts related to aging and older adults, below you will find a list of key terms and their definitions.

Key Terms and Definitions:

1. NBA Players: Refers to professional basketball players who have competed in the National Basketball Association (NBA), the premier men's basketball league in North America.

2. 7 Feet or Taller: Describes players who possess a height of at least 7 feet, indicating exceptional height and physical stature.

3. Retired: Indicates that the players discussed in the book are no longer active in professional basketball and have concluded their careers.

4. Towering Above the Rest: The title of the book, symbolizing the exceptional height of the players being featured and their prominence in the sport.

5. Basketball's Elite Big Men: Refers to the category of players known as "big men" in basketball, typically referring to those who play in the frontcourt positions (center and power forward) and are known for their size, strength, and dominance near the basket.

6. Fascination with Height in Basketball: Represents the intrigue and interest that surrounds tall players in the sport of basketball due to their unique physical attributes and the impact they have on the game.

7. Impact on the Game: Signifies the influence and effects that the featured players have had on the sport of basketball, including their contributions to team success, strategic considerations, and the overall development of the game.

8. Lesser-Known Tall Players: Refers to players who may not have achieved widespread recognition or fame despite their exceptional height, highlighting the focus of the book on exploring their stories and shedding light on their careers.

9. Giants: A term used to describe exceptionally tall basketball players, emphasizing their towering stature in comparison to the average height of players.

10. Legacy: Represents the lasting impact and contributions left by the featured players, including their records, achievements, and influence on subsequent generations of basketball players.

11. Challenges Faced: Denotes the obstacles and difficulties encountered by tall players, such as adapting to

their height, dealing with physical limitations, and facing unique expectations and pressures in the basketball world.

12. Basketball: The sport played on a rectangular court with two teams aiming to score points by shooting a ball through the opponent's hoop, using a combination of skill, strategy, and teamwork.

13. Non-fiction Book: A literary work that presents factual information and real-life events, in this case, focusing on the lives and careers of specific NBA players who meet the height and retirement criteria.

14. NBA: The National Basketball Association, the leading men's professional basketball league in North America, composed of teams from the United States and Canada.

Introduction

- Goldblatt, D. (2011). The Games: A Global History of the Olympics. W. W. Norton & Company.

- Rosen, C. (2004). The First Tip-Off: The Incredible Story of the Birth of the NBA. McGraw-Hill Education.

Chapter 1: Artis Gilmore - 7'2" - 1988

- Pluto, T. (2015). Loose Balls: The Short, Wild Life of the American Basketball Association. Simon and Schuster.

- Sachare, A. (1983). The Official NBA Basketball Encyclopedia. Villard.

Chapter 2: Frank Oleynick - 7'0" - 1976

- Borden, S. (2016). The Miracle of St. Anthony: A Season with Coach Bob Hurley and Basketball's Most Improbable Dynasty. Crown/Archetype.

- Haskins, J. (2016). Jayhawk: The Vii Foundation Presents. Sports Publishing.

Chapter 3: Gary Alcorn - 7'0" - 1962

- Tall Tales: The Glory Years of the NBA. (2000). Time-Life Books.

- Polinsky, R. (2019). Basketball Legends Are Born in May: Notebook Journal Composition Blank Lined Diary Notepad 120 Pages Paperback Black.

Chapter 4: Chuck Aleksinas - 7'0" - 1987

Supporting Materials

- Alexander, R. (2015). When Basketball Was Jewish: Voices of Those Who Played the Game. University of Nebraska Press.

- Reynolds, B. (2018). Basketball Junkie: A Memoir. Macmillan.

Chapter 5: Dave Newmark - 7'0" - 1972

- Cohen, J. (2013). Rockin' Steady: A Guide to Basketball and Cool. Simon and Schuster.

- Rosen, C. (2006). The Essence of the Game Is Deception: Thinking About Basketball. AuthorHouse.

Chapter 6: Stuart Gray - 7'1" - 1989

- Lazenby, R. (2016). Showboat: The Life of Kobe Bryant. Little, Brown.

- McCallum, J. (2017). Golden Days: West's Lakers, Steph's Warriors, and the California Dreamers Who Reinvented Basketball. Random House.

Conclusion

- McCallum, J. (2010). Dream Team: How Michael, Magic, Larry, Charles, and the Greatest Team of All Time Conquered the World and Changed the Game of Basketball Forever. Random House.

- Simmons, B. (2011). The Book of Basketball: The NBA According to The Sports Guy. ESPN Books.